Giorgio Agamben
What Is Fear?

Translated by Valeria Dani

ERIS
gems

WHAT *IS* FEAR, INTO WHICH PEOPLE today seem to have fallen so deeply that they have forgotten their ethical, political, and religious beliefs? It is surely something familiar and yet, at the same time, if we attempt to define it, it seems to obstinately evade comprehension.

In Par. 30 of *Being and Time*, Heidegger offers an exemplary discussion of fear as a mode of attunement. Fear can only be understood if we begin with the fact that *Dasein* (the term Heidegger uses to refer to the existential structure of man) is always already rooted in attunement—the latter describing Dasein's originary openness to the world. Since attunement is this originary openness to and discovery of the world, consciousness is always already anticipated by it. Consciousness can, therefore, neither dispense with attunement nor expect that it can master it. Attunement should not be confused with a psychological state—it is, ontologically, the openness that has always already shown man in his being-in-the-world-ness. Only through

3

attunement are experiences, affections, and knowledge possible: "reflection can find 'experiences' only because the there is already disclosed in attunement". A mood may assail us, yet "[i]t comes neither from 'without' nor from 'within', but rises from being-in-the-world itself as a mode of that being". However, this openness does not mean that what it is being revealed to is recognised as such. On the contrary, openness makes manifest just a naked facticity: "[t]he pure 'that it is' shows itself, the whence and the whither remain obscure". This is why Heidegger can say that attunement opens the *there* precisely in "the *thrownness* […]of […] being into its there". The openness that occurs in attunement is, in other words, a being-given-over to something that cannot be assumed and which it vainly attempts to escape.

This is evident in bad moods, in boredom, and in depression. Like any other attunement, they disclose Dasein "more primordially, but [they] also *close* […] it off more stubbornly, than any *not*-perceiving".

So, in depression, "Dasein becomes blind to itself, the surrounding world of heedfulness is veiled, the circumspection of taking care is led astray". Even in this case, however, Dasein is consigned to a disclosure from which it cannot possibly free itself.

It is in the context of this ontology of attunement that we should situate our analysis of fear. Heidegger starts by examining three aspects of that phenomenon: the 'before which' (*Wovor*) of fear, the 'fearing itself' (*Fürchten*), and the 'about which' (*Worum*) of fear. The 'before which', the object of fear, is always something intramundane. What is frightening is always—whatever its nature—something within the world and as such it has a dangerous and threatening nature. It can be more or less known and nonetheless "'unnerving' ['*geheuer*']", and it is placed within a determinate nearness however far away it is.

> As something threatening, what is harmful is not yet near enough to be dealt with, but

it is coming near. As it approaches, harmful-
ness radiates and thus has the character of
threatening. [...] As something approaches
in nearness [...] what is harmful is threatening, it can get us, and yet perhaps not. [...]
[W]hat is harmful, approaching near, bears
the revealed possibility of not happening
and passing us by. This does not lessen or
extinguish fearing, but enhances it.

(This 'certain uncertainty' which character-
ises fear is also evident in Spinoza's defini-
tion: an "intermittent pain [...] arising from
the image of a dubious event".)

As for the second characteristic of fear,
'fearing itself', Heidegger specifies that "[i]t
is not that we initially ascertain a future
evil (*malum futurum*) and then are afraid
of it". Rather, the fearsomeness of the thing
approaching us is discovered at the outset.

As a dormant possibility of attuned being-in-
the-world, fearing, 'fearfulness' has already
disclosed the world with regard to the fact

that something like a fearful thing can draw near to us from this fearfulness. The ability to draw near is itself freed by the essential, existential spatiality of being-in-the-world.

Fearfulness as originary disclosedness of Dasein always precedes any determinable fear.

Lastly, regarding that 'about which' fear is afraid, it is always the same being that feels fear, the Dasein, this determined man that is at question.

Only a being which is concerned in its being about that being can be afraid. Fearing discloses this being in its jeopardization, in its being left to itself.

Being afraid for our own house, for our property, or for others, does not challenge this diagnosis. It can be said that we are 'fearful' for someone else without our being truly scared, but if we actually feel afraid it *is* for ourselves, because we fear that the other could be "snatched away from us".

In this sense, fear is a fundamental mode of attunement that shows humans in their being as always already exposed and threatened. Naturally, this threat has different degrees: if something threatening, which is in front of us with its "not right now, but at any moment" character, suddenly hits this being, fear becomes alarm (*Erschrecken*); if what is threatening is not already known but is instead profoundly unfamiliar, fear becomes horror (*Grauen*). When something threatening combines both, then fear becomes terror (*Entsetzen*). In any case, all these different forms of attunement show that man, in his own disclosedness, is fundamentally fearful.

The only other attunement that Heidegger analyses in *Being and Time* is anxiety. And it is to anxiety, and not to fear, that the status of 'fundamental' attunement is attributed. But it is specifically in relation to fear that Heidegger is able to define the nature of anxiety, by determining at the outset "[h]ow [...] what anxiety is anxious about [is] phenomenally differentiated from what fear is afraid of [...]". While fear always has to do with *something*, "[w]hat anxiety is about is not an innerworldly being". Not only is the perceived threat potentially harmless, but

> [w]hat anxiety is about is completely indefinite. This indefiniteness not only leaves factically undecided which innerworldly being is threatening, it also means that innerworldly beings in general are not 'relevant' [...].

What anxiety is about is not a being, but the world as such. That is to say, anxiety is "the world in its worldliness":

> only because anxiety always already latently determines being-in-the-world, can being-in-the-world [...] be afraid. Fear is anxiety which has fallen prey to the 'world'. It is inauthentic and concealed from itself as such.

It has been rightly observed that the primacy of anxiety over fear affirmed by Heidegger can easily be reversed: instead of defining fear as a diminished anxiety which has fallen into an object, we can legitimately define anxiety as a fear deprived of its object. If the object is taken away from fear, fear is transformed into anxiety. In this sense, fear would then be the fundamental attunement into which man is already and always at risk of falling. Hence its essential political meaning—going back at least as far as Hobbes—which constitutes fear as that by which power is both established and justified.

Let's try to unpack and develop Heidegger's analysis. It is significant, in the present context, that fear always refers to a 'thing', to an intramundane being (in the present case to a virus, the tiniest of beings). Its intramundane nature means that it has lost any relation with openness to the world, and that it exists factitiously and inexorably without the possibility of transcendence. If the structure of being-in-the-world implies for Heidegger a transcendence and an openness, it is this same transcendence that delivers Dasein to the sphere of thinghood. Being-in-the-world means, in fact, being co-originally restored to the things that that openness to the world reveals. While the animal, without a world, cannot perceive an object as such, man, in opening to a world, can be assigned to a thing as a thing without escape.

This leads to the originary possibility of fear: it is the attunement disclosed when man, losing the nexus between the world and things, finds himself irremissibly consigned to intramundane beings and cannot figure out his relationship with a 'thing', which now becomes threatening. Once his relationship to the world is lost, the 'thing' becomes in itself terrorising. Fear is the dimension into which humanity falls when consigned, as has happened in modernity, to an unavoidable thingness. The fearsome being, the 'thing' that attacks and threatens people in horror movies, is thus nothing

11

more than an incarnation of this inescapable thingness.

This also brings out the feeling of impotence that defines fear. Those who feel fear try in every way and by every means to protect themselves from the thing that threatens them—by wearing a mask, for example, or by staying at home. This does not reassure them, however, but on the contrary renders their impotence against the 'thing' even more palpable and constant. Fear can in this light be defined as the opposite of the will to power. The essential character of fear is a will to impotence, a wanting-to-be-impotent in the face of the fearsome thing. Likewise, those who feel fear seek reassurance from those who are recognised as possessing some authority (doctors, civil protection officials, etc.), but this does not in any way get rid of the feeling of insecurity that accompanies fear—which is an essential element of the will to insecurity, the wanting-to-be-insecure. The truth of this is evident from the fact that the very subjects whose responsibility it is to reassure are those who, instead, perpetuate insecurity. They tirelessly repeat, for the good of the frightened, that the object of their fear can never be defeated or eliminated.

How is one to deal with this fundamental attunement, in which man seems always and constitutively to be in the act of collapsing? Since fear precedes and forestalls knowledge and reflection, it is quite useless to try and convince the frightened with rational arguments and evidence; more than anything, fear denies them access to a reasoning process that would preclude fear itself. As Heidegger writes, fear "bewilders us and makes us 'lose our heads'". So much so that, in the face of the epidemic, it was evident that the publication of irrefutable data and opinions from trustworthy sources was being systematically ignored and discarded in favour of others that, by the way, did not even feign scientific credibility.

Given the originary character of fear, the only way we can ever untangle it is by accessing an equally originary dimension. Such a dimension does exist: it is an openness to the world in which only things can appear and threaten us. Things become fearsome because we forget their co-belonging to a world that transcends them and, at the same time, makes them present. The only possibility of severing the 'thing' from the fear from which it seems inseparable lies in remembering that openness in which it has always and already been exposed and revealed. Not reasoning, but memory—remembering ourselves and our being-in-the-world—is what grants us again access to a thingness that is free from fear. This 'thing' that terrifies me, invisible to the eye though it is, is as open in its pure existence as are all other intramundane beings—this tree, this stream, this man. Only because I am in the world can things appear to me and, potentially, scare me. They are a part of my being-in-the-world, and it is this fact— rather than a thingness abstractly separate and wrongfully established as sovereign—

which dictates the ethical and political rules of my behaviour. Of course, the tree may break and fall on me, the stream can overflow and flood the town, and this man can unexpectedly hit me. If these contingencies materialise, a proportionate level of concern will dictate the appropriate course of action. No need to lose our heads, no need to let anyone exercise power on the basis of fear or, by transforming an emergency into a permanent state, to rewrite the rules that guarantee our freedom and determine what we can and cannot do.

All references to Heidegger are: Martin Heidegger, *Being and Time*, trans. Joan Stambaugh and Dennis J. Schmidt (Albany: State University of New York Press, 2010); and to Spinoza: Benedictus de Spinoza, *Spinoza's Ethics*, ed. Clare Carlisle, trans. George Eliot (Princeton: Princeton University Press, 2020), 178.

ERIS

265 Riverside Dr.
New York, NY 10025

"What Is Fear" originally appeared in the collec-
tion of essays, articles, and other interventions on
and about the COVID-19 pandemic *Where Are We
Now*, trans. Valeria Dani (London and New York:
ERIS, 2021), 107–14.

ISBN 978-1-967751-50-1

eris.press